UPON SECRECY

Selene Castrovilla

Illustrated by
Jeff Crosby and Shelley Ann Jackson

CALKINS CREEK

HONESDALE, PENNSYLVANIA

Lord, make me an instrument of Thy peace;
where there is hatred,
let me sow love.
—Prayer of St. Francis of Assisi

The author would like to thank the following people for their expertise:
Amy Northrop Adamo, director, Fraunces Tavern Museum, New York, New York
Andrew Batten, former director of Fraunces Tavern Museum and former executive director of
Raynham Hall Museum, Oyster Bay, New York
Al Casazza, Long Island historian and volunteer, Raynham Hall Museum
Dr. Gary Corrado, author and Revolutionary War historian
The staff of The David Library of the American Revolution, Washington Crossing, Pennsylvania
Beverly C. Tyler, Long Island historian, Three Village Historical Society, Setauket, New York

Thanks also to Pascale Laforest for her valuable assistance.

Calkins Creek
An Imprint of Boyds Mills Press, Inc.
815 Church Street
Honesdale, Pennsylvania 18431
Printed in China

Library of Congress Cataloging-in-Publication Data

Castrovilla, Selene.
Upon secrecy / Selene Castrovilla ; illustrated by Jeff Crosby and Shelley Ann Jackson. — 1st ed.
p. cm.
Includes bibliographical references.
ISBN 978-1-59078-573-7 (alk. paper)
1. United States—History—Revolution, 1775–1783—Secret service—Juvenile literature.
2. Washington, George, 1732–1799—Career in espionage—Juvenile literature. I. Crosby, Jeff, ill.
II. Jackson, Shelley, ill. III. Title.

E279.C37 2009
973.3'85—dc22

2009000946

Endsheet map courtesy of Clements Library, University of Michigan

First edition
The text of this book is set in 13-point Adobe Caslon.
The illustrations are done in acrylic.

10 9 8 7 6 5 4 3 2 1

For Lee and Nancy Feldman, Carolyn P. Yoder,
and my sons, Casey and Michael
—S.C.

For our brothers, Tim and Chris,
the spies with whom we grew up
— J.C. and S.A.J.

Introduction

The necessity of procuring good intelligence is apparent and need not be further urged. All that remains for me to add is, that you keep the whole matter as secret as possible. For upon secrecy, success depends. ...
—George Washington

GEORGE WASHINGTON NEEDED SPIES.

Information about the enemy was vital.

Learning British military plans was his only chance to level the advantage the redcoats held.

Washington's army had become something to reckon with. They'd gone from fighting for survival to spotting fear in their enemy's eyes.

Still, the British army was larger.

Better equipped.

Virtually impossible to outfight.

Washington knew that wits, not weapons, held the key to ultimate victory.

The general's problem wasn't finding information. Captured British soldiers often spilled secrets. Redcoats would appear on their own, prepared to turn traitor against their king. Even civilians offered to spy for a fee. But could Washington trust them?

A favorite tactic of Washington's was to slip false intelligence into enemy hands. The same could be done to him.

One mistake could mean defeat.

Washington also knew that his spies needed to live in or near New York—British headquarters. And they needed a good reason to be there.

The British were keen on protecting their territory, and New York was their biggest prize. People who didn't belong there were noticed.

In August 1778, Washington turned to Major Benjamin Tallmadge to organize what came to be called the Culper Spy Ring. A native of Setauket, Long Island, Tallmadge had the connections Washington needed and recruited longtime friends.

The heart of the ring lay with Robert Townsend, a New Yorker who wrote for a loyalist newspaper. Townsend was perfect for the job. British soldiers actually brought him information to see their names in print!

And Townsend was a Quaker.

Opposed to war.

Above suspicion.

For nearly two years the Culpers risked their lives smuggling letters.

Washington was impressed with Townsend's reports. But pleased as he was by their content, he grew irritated by the length of time it took to get them. Bluntly, he wrote to Tallmadge that the information was useless when it reached him.

Vexed, Washington disbanded the ring in May 1780.

But it didn't take long for Washington to miss Townsend's reliable messages. In July of that year, a French fleet of over five thousand troops was due to land in Newport, Rhode Island. Without this help, the Americans might well be doomed.

Washington worried.

Did the British know the French were coming?

He feared the worst.

The redcoats had the manpower to crush the French, especially if they struck before the fleet organized.

Washington needed information—from a source he could depend on.

There was only one.

Could the Culpers act fast enough?

He had to take the chance.

As we may every moment expect the arrival of the French fleet a revival of the correspondence with the Culpers will be of very great importance.
—George Washington to Benjamin Tallmadge, July 11, 1780

New York
July 20, 1780

GOD, *FORGIVE ME.*

The words flashed through Robert Townsend's mind like musket blasts against a dark sky.

They were there, always—when he squirmed in his chair at the offices of Rivington's *Royal Gazette*, when he sifted through inventory in his dry-goods store, when he shifted on his creaking bed in the black, dreamless night.

Over and over, the words blazed through his head. Uninvited, relentless—most especially now, in times like this. Sitting across from two British officers in his publisher's coffeehouse, taking notes on their exploits.

That was the purpose of this place—to gather every drop of gossip feasible and put it into print.

These soldiers thought they were sharing information with a journalist loyal to the crown. They craved recognition, even fame.

They had no idea to whom they were revealing themselves.

Forgive me, I beg of you.

He dared not pray that these words cease fire. Forsaking his Quaker faith to help the American cause, he'd known there would be suffering.

If there would be forgiveness, he did not know.

The soldier on the left droned on, competing with conversation and laughter at the surrounding tables. The workday had ended and the coffeehouse was packed. Cloudy tobacco smoke mixed with the scent of coffee. Chairs scraped across floor planks. Boots stomped, sweeping through scattered sawdust.

Robert stared at candle wax drip, drip, dripping, clotting onto the wood table. He didn't wish to look the men in their eyes. Almost on its own, his hand dipped quill into ink, then shifted back to the paper in front of him, scrawling notes of British military plans.

The plans.

They were what he was after.

One plan, specifically.

For four days he'd tramped around town, seeking the information. Did the British know about the French fleet landing in Newport?

He'd seen the British ships preparing to embark.

But to where?

Robert mustered a smile, forced his gaze at the officer on the right. Casually, he asked if either of them might know where the British fleet intended to sail. Posing such a question held risk, but time was paramount.

To these soldiers, he was Robert Townsend, reporter and merchant.

To General George Washington, he was known by code name only: Samuel Culper Junior.

Spy.

HE COULDN'T EVEN PACE.

Austin Roe wanted to move. He needed to let out this energy tingling inside, pressing him on, on, on ... but he had to stay still.

He couldn't so much as shift on the bed— it squeaked.

Austin didn't dare call attention to the triangular attic room in the boarding house where he hid. British officers inhabited most of the rooms beneath. They'd doubtless want to know why he was lurking in Robert Townsend's room.

It'd been nearly five days since he set out from Setauket, Long Island, urging his fastest horse through the night, galloping through fifty-five miles of forest to New York.

The note to Robert Townsend lay deep in his pouch.

Austin was supposed to be buying supplies for his Setauket tavern—that was his excuse for entering New York. But fetching supplies didn't take four days, and it didn't require staying at the home of the merchant whose shop he frequented.

Mercifully, the British didn't keep record of how long people stayed in New York. He'd be searched when he left—that's all.

So if he could sit still, things would be fine.

Just sit still and wait for Robert. Then he could move again.

He wasn't afraid to be a courier in a spy ring, carrying secret messages. He thrived on excitement— another kind of propulsion.

Stillness.

That was death.

Austin's eyes darted across the tiny room yet again, looking for something to occupy his restless mind. But there was nothing, almost nothing there at all. A desk with inkwell, quill, and paper neatly stacked. A chair. A washbasin. A mirror.

Robert Townsend lived simply, indeed.

That was a Quaker for you.

It smelled stale, the air felt so stifling. Austin focused on the ray of sun streaming steady and strong through the small round window. Oh, to be that light.

Or at least to be in it.

His legs were numb. He fidgeted ever slightly, then held back a curse as the bed s-s-s-creaked.

Motion, it was in his nature.

The door hinges squealed when Robert hurried in, nodding to Austin. He'd found out what they needed.

Austin stretched and hoisted his stiff self from the bed. Savoring the flow of blood through his twinging legs, he watched Robert take a vial from a pocket of one of his vests hanging in the closet. All Robert's vests were pitch-black, his shirts stark white. The shirt collars were tall and taut. Buttoned closed, they always seemed tethered to his neck.

Sitting at his desk, Robert gave his collar a hard tug. He smelled of tobacco, triggering fresh pangs inside Austin.

Robert opened the vial, stuck his quill in, then penned a message. What it said, Austin couldn't know, for the ink was invisible. It was called sympathetic stain.

When he finished, Robert sighed. He grabbed at his collar again, then flipped the page over. This time he dipped his quill in the inkwell, composing a false message from himself to Colonel Benjamin Floyd, a farmer on Long Island. The note said the supplies Floyd had requested weren't available. This ruse allowed Austin to slip out of New York with only the note—no heavy items weighing him down.

Robert folded the paper with two precise creases, inched back his chair in a low, scratchy sound, and stood. Austin reached for his wide-brimmed hat on the bed, fixed it on his head. Time for action, finally. Time to sneak down the stairs, past all those rooms of grim-hearted redcoats, back to his waiting steed.

Time to coolly fool the sentries guarding New York.

Time to brave the forest again, in all its dim elements.

Time to get back to Setauket.

Fast.

The edges of Austin's lips curved into a sly smile.

Fast was his way—the only way to live.

But Robert looked so grave. He pushed the page into Austin's hand, firm. Austin felt Robert's pulse beating through it.

Or maybe it was his own.

Austin nodded now, in farewell.

Anxious to move.

Thump, thump, thump …

Would the man never release his hand?

As if he'd heard Austin's thoughts, Robert let go.

His voice a crawling hush, he told Austin: "Godspeed."

11

Clack-clomping through the deep night over dirt, rock, and shell had been more jarring for Austin than usual. He'd spurred his horse on as never before and felt rather breathless.

Surprising, for him.

There was also the group of highway robbers who'd popped out of the thick woods and shot at him.

They missed.

'Cept they did get his hat.

He hadn't seen much of them—they were all a cussing blur.

But their gun bursts—those were pretty clear.

Extra speed was in fact a very good thing, he reckoned, when heading away from thieves with firearms.

He was back in Setauket now, almost done. And he had to admit: for once he'd be fine with slowing down for a piece.

After tying his horse to the fence, he knocked on Abraham Woodhull's farmhouse door. Woodhull was a stuttering, stammering, pasty-faced, ever-ailing, nervous wreck of a human. He'd been like that since Austin had known him, which was always.

They'd grown up together.

That Abe was also the spy for Washington called Samuel Culper Senior, well … Austin would've just about fallen over with laughter if anyone other than Abe had told him.

He nearly did anyway.

He wondered why Ben Tallmadge had chosen such a man for such a job, but then, that probably was why.

Austin banged hard.

Abe had been burning with fever last time Austin saw him, so Abe said.

Likely, he remained in bed, even five days later.

That was Abe for you.

The door groaned open. Abe appeared, bleary-eyed and sure enough in nightshirt and barefoot. He didn't look good. But with five days' growth on his face and little sleep to show for that time, Austin quite probably didn't look good either.

Abe glanced at the hole in Austin's hat but said nothing. They went inside.

Austin cast dust from his boots with each step.

Abe dragged his naked feet through the powdery dirt left behind.

At the table, Austin filled Abe in. He handed over the paper with Robert's invisible words. Abe's hands trembled. Abe blamed the shivering on his being sick, but he was endlessly shaking over something.

Quivering still, Abe pulled a jar from a drawer. He opened it, then dabbed at Robert's note with the clear liquid that was inside.

It looked like water.

Water, it wasn't.

Words appeared.

The two men scanned what Robert wrote. Austin's stomach tightened.

General Washington needed to see this.

Austin nearly lost patience with Abe, who was adding his own rambling message at the bottom, repeating things Robert had already said. Plus, he was going on about that fever of his.

What had that to do with anything?

Austin was about to ask him, when Abe finished.

On a separate sheet, Abe scribbled a note to Lieutenant Caleb Brewster. Caleb was the whaleboat captain who would ferry the message across Long Island Sound to Connecticut.

American territory.

He wrote: "Sir. The enclosed requires your immediate departure this day by all means let not an hour pass: for this day must not be lost. You have news of the greatest consequence perhaps that ever happened to your country."

Looking satisfied, though still twittering, Abe handed Austin the dispatches to forward to Caleb.

He coughed, hacked up a wad of phlegm, and spit.

Mission complete, Abe returned to bed.

Slamming the farmhouse door behind him, Austin started toward his horse.

Caleb Brewster skimmed over Abe's note to him and snorted. That Abe, he was amusing. Did he suppose Caleb would dawdle, stop for a spot of tea before setting off to the task of transporting Culper Junior's letter?

He'd never let a day slip from his grasp—not a minute.

Never.

Still, he'd have to forgo any British ships along the way. He did so relish those captures—such easy pickings. Of course, sometimes they fought back, then things got a wee bit complicated. He hadn't lost one yet, though.

No, on this trip he'd possess a single mind.

Get this note to Connecticut, or die trying. Get it into the hands of a courier who would rush it to General Washington.

Caleb sucked in a robust, salty breath. He wasn't aiming on dying, not today.

Caleb's men dozed in various nooks and crevices of the craggy cave they'd chosen to stow away in. A slew of snore tones chorused in the air, backdropped by the tumbling tide outside. At the center of the cavern lay their whaleboat—lugged across the shoreline into hiding. Its exterior was coated in gritty sand.

Caleb could relate.

He let out a long, low whistle—the signal to his crew to haul themselves up and out.

They hadn't a moment to lose.

IN HIS HEART, HE'D KNOWN.

Something in his soul had told George Washington: the British knew the French fleet was landing.

His instincts were correct.

He thumped—back, forth, back, forth—to the far ends of his headquarters, eyeing Culper Junior's dispatch again.

The facts were plain.

The British commander in chief, General Sir Henry Clinton, was sending eight thousand troops to ambush the French at Newport.

Washington ground his teeth.

This meant defeat.

Certainly for the French, who had three thousand fewer men and no time to organize their ranks. And nearly just as certain for the Americans, who couldn't hold on to their fight alone.

What could be done now?

There was one thing Clinton valued so highly that he would give his all to save it: New York. Taken as British headquarters at the start of the war.

He understood how Clinton felt. Recapturing New York would mean equally as much to Washington.

But Washington hadn't the manpower to launch such an operation.

Not by far.

Thud, thud, thud, thud …

He hoofed the floorboard edges.

His pacing seemed without resolution. So did his problem. He stared at pine knots in his walls, in his floor … knots, knots everywhere.

In his mind, that's all there was—knots.

And those British ships bounding through the waves, full sail.

Washington's focus landed at the quill on his desk.

The idea struck him.

He didn't need to attack. Clinton had only to believe that he intended to.

And Washington knew just how to convince him.

He crouched at his desk, setting to work. Rapidly, he produced detailed plans for a fictitious full-scale invasion of New York with twelve thousand men.

He couldn't help but smile, imagining Clinton's reaction when he saw them.

But the weight of the situation forced the grin from Washington's face.

Would Clinton be fooled?

It was up to God now.

New York
July 22, 1780

THE LIGHT FADED FROM SIR HENRY CLINTON'S EYES.

He'd had visions of crushing the French, of finally bringing this bloody war to an end.

Who could have thought a simple farmer would change all that?

A farmer, delivering a packet he'd discovered along the highway.

Lost in the mud.

Someone had dropped it. Thank God. For in that packet was the most distressing sight he'd ever seen: a mapped-out proposal to attack New York!

Heavens!

He swiped the perspiration beading at his temple. Doubtless, Washington had learned that Clinton's fleet was embarking.

Washington was ready to take full advantage of its absence.

Clinton felt his blood drain at the thought of it.

Oh, but George Washington had a surprise coming.

Forget Newport. Forget the French.

Clinton wasn't losing New York—his most precious asset!

But his fleet was sailing along Long Island—at full mast. What could he do?

Clinton's heart was in a flutter. With haste, he scripted the orders. A series of fires would be set along the shore. This chain would continue until it reached the ships—alerting them to abandon their course.

They were to turn around immediately.

Return and mount a defense of New York.

Clinton prayed they would make it in time.

Little did Sir Henry Clinton suspect that George Washington's prayers had just been answered.

Washington did not really outfight the British; he simply outspied us!
—Major George Beckwith, head of British intelligence operations
in the colonies at the end of the war

Afterword

Sir Henry Clinton never learned that he'd been duped. When the attack on New York didn't happen, he merely thought that Washington had seen the ships return and changed his mind.

Townsend's letter with the Newport information was the fastest dispatch ever delivered by the Culpers—and this success restored Washington's faith in his spies. He later wrote, "Of the Culpers fidelity and ability I entertain the highest opinion."

The Culpers continued to serve for the war's duration.

Victory met, Washington later took a tour of Long Island. He made sure to stop in Setauket to thank his spies.

Washington also visited Oyster Bay, Long Island.

He couldn't know it, but his most trusted spy lived there. Robert Townsend never revealed himself to Washington, or anyone else. The few people aware of his identity—Abraham Woodhull and the ring's couriers—respected Townsend's privacy.

The Quaker was too filled with guilt and shame to ever admit his crucial role in the Revolutionary War. He went to his grave unacknowledged.

Townsend's identity remained a mystery until 1930. That's when Long Island historian Morton Pennypacker made a startling discovery: merchant and reporter Robert Townsend shared the same handwriting as Samuel Culper Junior.

How Did the British Know?

Washington's anxieties about what the British knew proved to be well founded. What he didn't imagine was how Sir Henry Clinton had found out the French were coming.

One of the men closest to Washington had also become adept in espionage—for the other side. General Benedict Arnold had been corresponding with Clinton's chief of intelligence, Major John André, since April 1779, and he'd embraced the opportunity to prove himself by providing important data.

The traitorous Arnold wasted no time betraying Washington. He'd dispatched a coded message to André about Newport on June 12, 1780, the same evening that Washington confided in him. Washington never suspected that the letter exposing the arrival of the French came straight from his own headquarters in Morristown, New Jersey, penned by his bravest, most beloved general and delivered by secret courier into Clinton's eager grasp.

Arnold's second try at treason came that fall. He plotted to surrender West Point—a key American fort on the Hudson River under his command—to the British. He intended also to surrender Washington himself, who would be visiting the fort at Arnold's request. The plan was thwarted when Major André was accosted by highway robbers as he returned to New York from a meeting with Arnold. He had a map of West Point hidden in his boot. Seeing this, the thieves turned André in to the Americans for a reward.

But the Americans didn't realize the true significance of their prisoner. Not suspecting Arnold, they were about to send André back to West Point, into Arnold's custody. Luckily, one person pieced together Arnold's treachery and ordered André held back. It was Washington's chief of intelligence, Major Benjamin Tallmadge.

About "Sympathetic Stain"

It is too great a risque to write with ink in this country of robbers.
I this day just saved my life. ... I was attacked by four armed men. ... They
searched every pocket and lining of my clothes, shoes, and also my saddle,
which the enclosed was in, but thank kind Providence they did not find it.

—Abraham Woodhull

With good reason, Abraham Woodhull was nervous about writing messages to George Washington. It was a great relief when Washington received a gift of the invisible ink called "sympathetic stain" (together with the substance that would make the ink visible again) in November 1778. The stain came from John Jay, a member of the Continental Congress. Sir James Jay, John's brother, had invented it three years earlier in England. Washington wrote Benjamin Tallmadge: "I should be glad to have an interview with Culper myself, in which I would put the mode of corresponding upon such a footing that even if his letters were to fall into the enemy's hands, he would have nothing to fear, on that account."

Unfortunately, possessing a "magical" solution didn't prevent human error. Not long after receiving the stain, Abraham knocked over the vial, spilling it all.

Waiting for Sir James to send more stain from England, the Culpers used an elaborate code system Benjamin had devised, substituting numbers for words. But instead of taking the time to encode his entire letters, Abraham only used the code for certain words.

This made the messages easy for anyone to decipher, and it made Washington livid. Fortunately, more stain was available when the Culpers needed to pass on the information about Newport.

Washington also found fault at times with stained notes, writing to Tallmadge: "C-r, Jr. should avoid making use of the Stain upon a blank sheet of paper (which is the usual way of its coming to me). This circumstance alone is sufficient to raise suspicions. A much better way is to write a letter in the Tory stile with some mixture of family matters and between the lines and on the remaining part of the sheet communicate with the stain the intended intelligence."

After the War

Robert Townsend returned to his family's newly liberated home in Oyster Bay, Long Island. It had been taken over by a British regiment called the Queen's Rangers and used as their headquarters during the war. He remained in that same house with his sisters until his death on March 7, 1838, at age eighty-four. He died as he'd lived, in quiet obscurity.

Austin Roe joined the Suffolk County militia regiment after the war. He moved to Patchogue, Long Island, in 1798 and opened Roe's Hotel. He died there in 1830 at age eighty-one.

Abraham Woodhull remained in Setauket, becoming the first judge of Suffolk County, Long Island. He died at age seventy-three on January 23, 1826.

Near the end of the war—in early December 1782— the daring Caleb Brewster received a grave injury during a battle at sea. Benjamin Tallmadge was there and later recorded the incident in his memoir: "On the first fire, every man in one of the enemy's boats fell, either being killed or wounded. Capt. Brewster received a ball in his breast, which passed through his body. He, however, captured two boats, and one escaped. Although we supposed Capt. Brewster mortally wounded, yet he recovered, and lived to be nearly 80 years old."

Caleb moved to Fairfield, Connecticut, after the war, becoming a blacksmith and then joining the forerunner of the Coast Guard in 1793. He died on his farm in Black Rock, Connecticut, on February 13, 1827.

Benjamin Tallmadge, who led the Culper Ring under George Washington while also heading his own troop of light dragoons (a regiment in which all the men rode horses) and conducting whaleboat raids across Long Island Sound, returned to his hometown of Setauket one more time after the war. He described the visit in his memoir: "The people had determined that they would celebrate the occasion by some public demonstration of their joy. They therefore concluded … they would have an ox roasted whole on the public green, to partake of which all were invited to attend. … The aged and the young, the male and the female, rejoiced to receive a portion which, from the novelty of the scene, and being in commemoration of so great an event, obtained a peculiar zest. All was harmony and joy, for all seemed to be of one mind. A Tory could not have lived in that atmosphere one minute. By sunset the whole concourse—a vast multitude—dispersed and returned to their own homes in quietness and peace."

Benjamin settled in Litchfield, Connecticut, where he became a successful businessman. He also served in the U.S. House of Representatives from 1801 to 1817. He died on March 7, 1835, at age eighty-one.

Author's Note

Writing about the Culpers proved challenging, because of their secretive nature. After the war, no one in the ring gave accounts of his experiences. Benjamin Tallmadge wrote a memoir but left out any specific mention of his role as spy. Robert Townsend never revealed his identity at all.

Historians were left to patch a timeline of the Culpers through their coded and often cryptic letters—and not all the letters made it through the war.

Then there were the tantalizing stories about the ring, passed down through time. Anna Strong Smith was a Setauket resident who reportedly had hung petticoats on her clothesline signaling when and where Caleb Brewster lay in wait. Although a juicy aspect to the Culper saga—and ironically the spark that ignited my quest to learn about the Culpers— Anna's involvement is pure speculation. Another Culper rumor is the participation of a mysterious woman in New York with whom Robert Townsend may have fallen in love. So intriguing and yet impossible to prove.

All this made it difficult to produce a lucid narrative. I struggled with the task for years. When my editor suggested I concentrate on the Newport incident, my story came together. Not only were all the facts known about this harrowing moment in history, but it was also the Culpers' finest achievement.

Nonfiction or fiction?

The historical event portrayed in this book happened. The struggles were real—both outer and inner.

The people are depicted in keeping with their character. Can I prove specific thoughts? No. But the states of mind I've described carry the weight of the situation they were thrust into—the burden placed on them to set aside their lives and all other commitments and beliefs in order to serve their country.

I give you truth—truth in history, truth in existence—presented as story, full of tension, detail, and momentum.

Timeline

1775 April: The battles of Lexington and Concord take place. The Battle of Breed's Hill follows in June.

1776 July 4: The Declaration of Independence is adopted. The war officially begins.

August 27: The Battle of Long Island is fought.

September 16: The British defeat Washington's troops at the Battle of Harlem Heights.

December 25: Washington and his men cross the Delaware River. The next day they capture Trenton, New Jersey.

1777 January 3: Washington wins the Battle of Princeton in New Jersey.

January 6–May 28: Washington and his troops winter in Morristown, New Jersey.

October 17: American troops defeat the British at the Battle of Saratoga.

December 19: Washington settles his troops at Valley Forge, Pennsylvania, for a brutal winter. They remain there until June 19, 1778.

1778 June 28: Washington fights the British to a draw at the Battle of Monmouth.

August: At Washington's request, Tallmadge organizes and heads (under Washington) the Culper Spy Ring.

1780 July: The Culper Spy Ring gives George Washington the information he needs to save the French fleet at Newport.

1781 October 19: British general Cornwallis surrenders at Yorktown, Virginia.

1783 September 3: The Treaty of Paris is signed. The long war is over.

Places to Visit

Bronx, New York
Valentine–Varian House—3266 Bainbridge Avenue.

Site of six skirmishes between American troops and the British forces who occupied the house for most of the Revolutionary War.

Van Cortlandt House—Van Cortlandt Park, Broadway at West 246th Street.

Site of numerous military encampments by both the Americans and the British. Washington set up headquarters in the house in 1776 and again in 1783. For much of the war, Van Cortlandt House sat in "no-man's land"—territory between the British in New York City and American troops to the north.

Long Island, New York
Earle–Wightman House—20 Summit Street, Oyster Bay.

Housing the Oyster Bay Historical Society, this site features a one-room house from colonial times.

East Hampton Public Library, the Long Island Collection—159 Main Street, East Hampton.

Excellent source for researching the Revolutionary period on Long Island.

Raynham Hall Museum—20 West Main Street, Oyster Bay.

The Townsend family homestead was the site of British headquarters in Oyster Bay during the Revolutionary War. Little did the British know that one member of the Townsend family was also Washington's most trusted spy.

Rock Hall Museum—199 Broadway, Lawrence.
Sands-Willets House—336 Port Washington Boulevard, Port Washington.

Dating back to the early 1700s, these houses now serve as museums.

Roe Tavern—Intersection of Route 25A and Bayview Avenue, East Setauket.

A state marker here designates this as the site of Austin Roe's tavern.

Setauket Elementary School—134 Main Street, East Setauket.

A polychrome statue of Benjamin Tallmadge, along with a plaque listing his accomplishments, stands in front of the gymnasium entrance. Inside the school are murals by artist Vance Locke that depict Setauket history, including the Culper Spy Ring in action.

Setauket Presbyterian Church—The Village Green, 5 Caroline Avenue, Setauket.

The grave of Abraham Woodhull is located here. Just a mile away, on Dyke Road, is a state marker at the spot where Woodhull's home stood. Group tours available.

Manhattan, New York
Fraunces Tavern Museum—54 Pearl Street.

Site where Washington gave his farewell address to his troops in 1783. The tavern also served as a meeting place for pre-Revolutionary activities. Read Benjamin Tallmadge's description of Washington's farewell, on permanent display, along with interesting memorabilia from the war as well as changing exhibitions on Revolutionary War themes.

Morris-Jumel Mansion—65 Jumel Terrace.

Washington's headquarters in September and October of 1776. Later used by the British.

Morristown, New Jersey
Morristown National Historical Park—30 Washington Place.

Visit Ford Mansion, Washington's headquarters during the winter of 1779–1780. It was here that Benedict Arnold dined as Washington's guest, learned the French were landing at Newport, and sent the information to the British.

Mount Vernon, Virginia
George Washington's Mount Vernon Estate and Gardens—3200 Mount Vernon Memorial Highway.

Visit George Washington's beloved home, where he farmed and lived with his wife, Martha, for more than forty years.

Newport, Rhode Island
King Park/Newport Harbor.

Visit the site where the French fleet landed in July 1780. The park is home to the Rochambeau statue—a tribute to the Compte de Rochambeau, leader of the French troops.

Washington, D.C.
International Spy Museum—800 F Street, NW.

Learn about the history of spying in this comprehensive collection.

Selected Bibliography

Papers (Primary Sources)

George Washington Papers at the Library of Congress, 1741–1799.

Henry Clinton Papers, William L. Clements Library, University of Michigan.

Thomas Jefferson Papers at the Library of Congress.

Townsend Family Papers, Raynham Hall Museum.

Newspapers (Primary Sources)

Pennsylvania Gazette.

Rivington's New-York Loyal Gazette and *The Royal Gazette.*

Books

Alden, John R. *George Washington: A Biography.* Baton Rouge: Louisiana State University Press, 1984.

Bakeless, John. *Turncoats, Traitors, and Heroes.* Philadelphia: J. B. Lippincott, 1959.

Bakeless, Katherine, and John Bakeless. *Spies of the Revolution.* Philadelphia: J. B. Lippincott, 1962.

Chase, Philander D., ed. *The Papers of George Washington.* Revolutionary War Series. 14 vols. Charlottesville: University of Virginia Press, 1985–2008.

Ferling, John E. *The First of Men: A Life of George Washington.* Knoxville: University of Tennessee Press, 1988.

Fitzpatrick, John C., ed. *The Diaries of George Washington, 1748–1799.* Vol. 2, 1771–1785. Vol. 4, 1789–1799. Boston: Houghton Mifflin, 1925.

Flexner, James Thomas. *George Washington in the American Revolution, 1775–1783.* Boston: Little, Brown, 1968.

Flexner, James Thomas. *The Traitor and the Spy: Benedict Arnold and John André.* Boston: Little, Brown, 1953.

Flexner, James Thomas. *Washington: The Indispensable Man.* Boston: Little, Brown, 1974.

Force, P., ed. *American Archives.* 4th and 5th ser., 1848–1853. Washington, DC.

Ford, Corey. *A Peculiar Service.* Boston: Little, Brown, 1965.

Freeman, Douglas Southall. *George Washington: A Biography.* Vol. 5, *Victory with the Help of France.* New York: Charles Scribner's Sons, 1952.

Graydon, Alexander. *Memoirs of His Own Time.* Edited by John Stockton Littell. Philadelphia: Lindsay and Blakiston, 1846.

Groh, Lynn. *The Culper Spy Ring.* Philadelphia: Westminster Press, 1969.

Jackson, Donald, and Dorothy Twohig, eds. *The Diaries of George Washington.* Charlottesville: University of Virginia Press, 1976–1979.

Jay, John. *The Correspondence and Public Papers of John Jay, 1763-1826.* Edited by Henry P. Johnston. New York: Da Capo Press, 1971.

Kinnaird, Clark. *George Washington: The Pictorial Biography.* New York: Bonanza Books, 1967.

Newsday. *Long Island, Our Story: The Celebrated Series.* Melville, NY: Newsday, 1998.

Old, Wendie C. *George Washington.* Springfield, NJ: Enslow Publishers, 1997.

Pennypacker, Morton. *General Washington's Spies on Long Island and in New York.* Brooklyn, NY: Long Island Historical Society, 1939.

Pennypacker, Morton. *The Two Spies.* Boston: Houghton Mifflin, 1930.

Scharf, J. Thomas. *History of Westchester County, New York: Including Morrisania, Kings Bridge, and West Farms....* Vol. 2. Philadelphia: L. E. Preston, 1886.

Tallmadge, Benjamin. *Memoir of Colonel Benjamin Tallmadge, Prepared by Himself....* New York: T. Holman, 1858.

Van Doren, Carl. *Secret History of the American Revolution: An Account of the Conspiracies of Benedict Arnold....* New York: Viking Press, 1941.

Articles

Fleming, T. "George Washington, Spymaster." *American Heritage*, February–March 2000.

Gilgoff, Dan. "Washington's Web." *U.S. News & World Report*, January 27, 2003.

Johnston, H. P. "The Secret Service of the Revolution." *Magazine of American History* 8, no. 2, February 1882.

Patrick, L. S. "The Secret Service of the American Revolution." *Journal of American History*, no. 1 (1907).

Tyler, Beverly C. "The Setauket Spies." *The Three Village Historical Society*, 2001.

Additional Sources

Brooklyn Public Library, Brooklyn, New York.

The David Library of the American Revolution, Washington Crossing, Pennsylvania.

East Hampton Public Library, East Hampton, New York.

Fraunces Tavern Museum, New York, New York.

New-York Historical Society, New York, New York.

New York Public Library, New York, New York.

Oyster Bay Historical Society, housed in the Earle Wightman House, Oyster Bay, Long Island.

Raynham Hall Museum, Oyster Bay, Long Island.

Three Village Historical Society, Setauket, Long Island.

Washington's Headquarters, Morristown, New Jersey.

White Plains Historical Society, White Plains, New York.

About the Art Research

In researching the illustrations for *Upon Secrecy*, we used many resources. For the uniforms, dress and gear, we referred mainly to books on the American Revolutionary War. For the settings, we visited historical sites in New York City, such as the Dyckman Farmhouse and Fraunces Tavern. To depict the characters, we consulted their portraits painted during their lifetimes, which we found in books and on the Internet. We also photographed ourselves and our family as models to accurately depict the poses and lighting of the figures.

Our illustrations for *Upon Secrecy* were reviewed for accuracy by Andrew Batten, former director of Fraunces Tavern Museum, New York, New York, and former executive director of Raynham Hall Museum, Oyster Bay, New York; and Beverly C. Tyler, Long Island historian, Three Village Historical Society, Setauket, New York.

Our paintings are done in acrylic on gessoed watercolor paper.

—*J.C. and S.A.J.*

LONG I

SEATON'S NECK

BR

Church

Meeting

Baylies Tavern